30 MINUTES OR LESS | Favourite Food

30
MINUTES
OR LESS

Favourite
Food

p

This is a Parragon Book

First published in 2006

Parragon

Queen Street House

4 Queen Street

Bath BA1 1HE, UK

ISBN: 1-40547-382-7

Printed in China

Produced by the Bridgewater Book Company Ltd

Front cover photography by Mike Cooper
Front cover home economy by Sumi Glass

Notes for the Reader

This book uses metric and imperial measurements. Follow the same units of measurement
throughout; do not mix metric and imperial. All spoon measurements are level: teaspoons are
assumed to be 5 ml, and tablespoons are assumed to be 15 ml. Unless otherwise stated,
milk is assumed to be full fat, eggs and individual vegetables are medium and pepper is
freshly ground black pepper.

Recipes using raw or very lightly cooked eggs should be avoided by children, the elderly,
pregnant women, convalescents and anyone suffering from an illness. Pregnant women and
breast-feeding women are advised to avoid eating peanuts and peanut products.

Contents

Introduction

Anyone who regularly cooks for themselves, family or friends will have asked the question 'What am I going to cook tonight?' The hard part is coming up with recipe ideas in the first place, and even your favourite meal can lose its appeal when it's in constant rotation.

EASE AND INSPIRATION

Written for everyone who loves food, these easy recipes have been specially chosen so that even the busiest person can cook their favourite food at home, and quickly, too. The book is organized into four recipe chapters: starters and snacks, main courses, accompaniments and light meals, and desserts. These offer tasty and imaginative suggestions for satisfying family suppers as well as stylish dinner parties, all requiring the minimum of time and effort. Recipes include favourite foods from around the world, from Asia to Mexico, with many well-loved stops along the way. There are traditional favourites, from Croque Monsieur and Garlic Bread to Pepper Steak and Caesar Salad, but you'll also find that many of these have been given a contemporary twist, being low in saturated fats and low in sugars for healthy and enjoyable eating.

All of the recipes in this book can be completed in 30 minutes or less – so there will be no need to slave away in the kitchen for hours upon end to make your favourite food. There are no complicated cooking methods or elaborate presentations, nor will you need to use every pot and pan in the kitchen. Simple step-by-step instructions and full-colour photographs enable even the most inexperienced to cook with confidence and success.

If you're tired of serving up the same old meals day in, day out, bored with staring at the contents of your refrigerator, seeking inspiration, and you simply long for favourite recipes that are quick, healthy and hassle-free, then look no further. These flavour-packed meals will satisfy your appetite as well as your taste buds and renew your enthusiasm for cooking. Achievable for anyone with a good knife and a few well-chosen pots and pans, you'll never have an excuse for being in a culinary rut again.

TOP TIPS FOR TIME MANAGEMENT

Follow these handy hints to be sure of making the most of the time you spend in the kitchen.

PLANNING

This is absolutely essential if you want to be efficient.

▸ Plan a week's menu and compile your shopping list from your recipes.

▸ Consider what's going on during the week – if you'll be out all day, forget doing a complicated meal like lasagne.

▸ Cook for the freezer – particularly with items like home-made tomato sauce for Italian dishes.

▸ Plan to have leftovers – a roast chicken one day can mean a stir-fry or soup on another day.

▸ Keep a good stock in your storecupboard and refrigerator of basic but versatile staples that can be dressed up or down as the need or your mood requires – rice, pasta, canned tomatoes, frozen meat and fish, frozen vegetables and cheese are a good place to start.

▸ Don't wait until something runs out before you replace it – whenever you find something is three-quarters empty, put it on your shopping list and buy more (keep a notepad on the front of the refrigerator, if it helps).

▸ Read through the recipe before starting so that you can assemble your ingredients and all the kitchen equipment you'll need.

SORT, PURGE AND ARRANGE

Clear worktops and clean out drawers, shelves and cupboards. Throw out or give away anything you don't use. Position the most frequently used items nearest the work area where they will be utilized, along with the other items they work with – this will prevent you wasting time and energy traipsing back and forth across the kitchen and it will make your cooking activities more efficient.

Don't forget to clean up as you go along. Many people avoid cooking primarily because they simply can't face the thought of the mess left at the end of the process. But if you put dirty utensils in the dishwasher or washbasin along the way, soak pans when necessary and mop up spills when they occur, the entire kitchen experience becomes more enjoyable and less time consuming.

Chapter One
Starters
and Snacks

Croque Monsieur
25 minutes to the table

MAKES 2

ingredients

85 g/3 oz Gruyère or Emmenthal
   cheese, grated
4 slices white bread, crusts removed
2 thick slices lean ham
1 small egg
about 40 g/1½ oz unsalted butter

CHEESE SAUCE
25 g/1 oz unsalted butter
1 tsp sunflower oil
½ tbsp plain flour
125 ml/4 fl oz warm milk
25 g/1 oz Gruyère or Emmenthal
   cheese, grated
pepper

method

Spread half the grated cheese on 2 slices of the bread, then top each with a slice of ham, cut to fit. Sprinkle the ham with the remaining cheese, then top with the remaining slices of bread and press down.

To make the cheese sauce, melt the butter with the oil in a small, heavy-based saucepan over a medium heat. Stir in the flour until well combined and smooth. Cook, stirring constantly, for 1 minute. Remove from the heat and stir in a little of the milk until well incorporated. Return to the heat and gradually add the remaining milk, stirring constantly. Cook, stirring, for a further 3 minutes, or until the sauce is smooth and thickened. Remove from the heat and stir in the cheese and pepper to taste, then set aside and keep warm.

Beat the egg in a soup plate or other flat bowl. Add 1 sandwich and press down to coat on both sides, then remove from the bowl and repeat with the other sandwich.

Preheat the grill to high. Line a baking tray with foil and set aside. Melt the butter in a sauté or frying pan over a medium-high heat. Add 1 or both sandwiches, depending on the size of your pan, and cook until golden brown on both sides. Add a little extra butter, if necessary, if you have to fry the sandwiches separately.

Transfer the sandwiches to the foil-lined baking tray and spread the cheese sauce over the top. Cook under the grill, about 10 cm/4 inches from the heat, for 4 minutes, or until golden and brown. Cut each sandwich in half diagonally and serve immediately.

Eggs Benedict with Quick Hollandaise Sauce

15 minutes to the table

SERVES 4

ingredients

1 tbsp white wine vinegar
4 eggs
4 English muffins
4 slices lean ham

QUICK HOLLANDAISE SAUCE
3 egg yolks
200 g/7 oz butter
1 tbsp lemon juice
pepper

method

Fill a wide frying pan three-quarters full with water and bring to the boil over a low heat. Reduce the heat to a simmer and add the vinegar. When the water is barely simmering, carefully break the eggs into the frying pan. Leave for 1 minute, then, using a large spoon, gently loosen the eggs from the bottom of the frying pan. Leave to cook for a further 3 minutes, or until the white is cooked and the yolk is still soft, basting the top of the egg with the water from time to time.

Meanwhile, to make the hollandaise sauce, put the egg yolks in a food processor or blender. Melt the butter in a small saucepan until bubbling. Gradually add the hot butter in a steady stream through the feeder tube of the food processor or blender until the sauce is thick and creamy. Add the lemon juice, and a little warm water if the sauce is too thick, then season to taste with pepper. Remove from the food processor or blender and keep warm.

Split the muffins and toast them on both sides. To serve, top each muffin with a slice of ham, a poached egg and a generous spoonful of the hollandaise sauce.

caution

Recipes using raw eggs should be avoided by infants, the elderly, pregnant women, convalescents and anyone suffering from an illness.

Brunch Bruschetta
10 minutes to the table

method

Toast the ciabatta bread.

Mix the tomato, spring onions, mozzarella cheese, avocado, balsamic vinegar and half the oil together in a bowl. Season to taste with salt and pepper.

Drizzle the remaining oil over the ciabatta toast and top with the tomato mixture.

Garnish with the basil and serve immediately.

SERVES 2

ingredients

4 slices ciabatta bread

1 large ripe tomato, diced

2 spring onions, finely sliced

1 small fresh buffalo mozzarella cheese, diced

½ ripe avocado, peeled, stoned and diced

½ tbsp balsamic vinegar

2 tbsp extra-virgin olive oil

salt and pepper

2 tbsp shredded fresh basil leaves, to garnish

Hummus
10 minutes to the table

SERVES 8

ingredients

450 g/1 lb canned chickpeas
juice of 2 large lemons
150 ml/5 fl oz tahini
2 garlic cloves, crushed
4 tbsp extra-virgin olive oil
small pinch of ground cumin
salt and pepper

TO GARNISH
1 tsp paprika
chopped fresh flat-leaf parsley

TO SERVE
warm pitta bread
green olives (optional)

method

Drain the chickpeas, reserving a little of the can liquid, and put in a food processor or blender. Process until smooth, gradually adding the lemon juice and enough of the reserved liquid to form a smooth, thick purée. Add the tahini, garlic, 3 tablespoons of the oil and the cumin and process again until smooth. Season to taste with salt and pepper.

Turn the mixture into a shallow serving dish, cover and leave to chill in the refrigerator until ready to serve.

To serve, mix the remaining oil with the paprika and drizzle over the top of the dip. Sprinkle with chopped parsley and accompany with warm pitta bread and olives, if you like.

Broccoli and Stilton Soup

30 minutes to the table

method

Heat the butter in a large saucepan over a medium heat. Add the onions and cook, stirring frequently, for 5-8 minutes, or until softened. Stir in the potato, then add the hot stock and bring to the boil. Reduce the heat and simmer for 5 minutes.

Add the broccoli and cook, stirring occasionally, for a further 5 minutes. Season to taste with pepper. Transfer the soup to a food processor or blender, in batches, and process until smooth. Return to a clean saucepan.

Add 150 ml/5 fl oz of the cream and 150 g/5½ oz of the cheese to the soup and cook over a low heat, stirring, until the cheese has melted.

Mash the remaining cheese with the remaining cream in a bowl.

Serve the soup hot in individual warmed bowls with the cream and cheese mixture, sprinkled with a few chives.

variation

To make Stilton croûtes to serve with the soup, brush slices of a baguette with olive oil and toast in a low oven until golden. Mash the Stilton cheese with only 1 tablespoon of double cream and spread onto the toasted bread. Float a croûte in each bowl of soup.

SERVES 4

ingredients

50 g/1¾ oz butter

2 onions, chopped

1 potato, peeled and diced

1 litre/1¾ pints hot vegetable or chicken stock

1 broccoli crown, broken into small florets

200 ml/7 fl oz double cream

200 g/7 oz Stilton or other firm blue cheese, crumbled

pepper

10 g/¼ oz fresh chives, snipped, to garnish

Gazpacho
15 minutes to the table

SERVES 4

ingredients

1 kg/2 lb 4 oz ripe tomatoes, peeled,
    deseeded and roughly chopped
½ cucumber, peeled, deseeded and
    roughly chopped
1 green pepper, deseeded and roughly
    chopped
115 g/4 oz fresh bread, crusts
    removed
1 small onion, roughly chopped
1 garlic clove, chopped
1 tbsp white wine vinegar
125 ml/4 fl oz olive oil
salt

TO GARNISH

small amount of tomatoes, cucumber
    and green pepper mixture
few fresh basil sprigs

TO SERVE

ice cubes
fresh crusty bread

method

Set aside some of the tomatoes, cucumber and green pepper for a
garnish. Put the bread into a food processor and process until crumbs
form. Add the remaining tomatoes, cucumber and green pepper, the
onion, garlic, vinegar and oil and process until smooth.

The tomatoes should have enough juice in them to make enough
liquid, but add a little water if the soup is too thick. Season to taste
with salt.

Divide the soup between 4 serving bowls and add a few ice cubes to
make sure that the soup is served chilled. Garnish with the reserved
tomatoes, cucumber and green pepper. Add a few basil sprigs and
serve with fresh crusty bread.

Pan-fried Scallops and Prawns

20 minutes to the table

SERVES 4

ingredients

12 shucked, cleaned raw scallops,
    thawed if frozen (see cook's tip)
12 raw large prawns, peeled
    and deveined
2 tbsp plain flour
3 tbsp olive oil
2 garlic cloves, finely chopped
2 tbsp chopped fresh parsley
3 tbsp lemon juice
salt and pepper

method

Using a sharp knife, cut the scallops in half, then season the scallops
and prawns to taste with salt and pepper. Spread the flour out on a
plate. Coat the scallops and prawns in the flour, shaking off any excess.

Heat the oil in a large, heavy-based frying pan over a medium heat.
Add the scallops and prawns and cook, turning once, for 2 minutes. Add
the garlic and parsley, then stir well, tossing the shellfish to coat, and
cook, shaking the frying pan occasionally, for 2 minutes, or until the
scallops are opaque and the prawns have turned pink.

Add the lemon juice and toss well to coat. Transfer to warmed plates
and serve immediately.

cook's tip

If using frozen scallops, thaw out slowly in the refrigerator. Once they
are completely thawed out, use immediately, or keep in the refrigerator
until ready to cook but use on the same day.

Baked Eggs with Spinach

30 minutes to the table

method

Preheat the oven to 200°C/400°F/Gas Mark 6.

Heat the oil in a frying pan over a medium heat. Add the shallots and cook, stirring frequently, for 4–5 minutes, or until softened. Add the spinach, cover and cook for 2–3 minutes, or until the spinach has just wilted. Remove the lid and cook until all the liquid has evaporated.

Add the cream to the spinach mixture and season to taste with nutmeg and pepper. Spread the spinach mixture over the base of a shallow gratin dish, then make 4 wells in the mixture with the back of a spoon.

Crack an egg into each well and scatter over the Parmesan cheese. Bake in the preheated oven for 12–15 minutes, or until the eggs are set. Serve with toasted Granary bread.

SERVES 4

ingredients

1 tbsp olive oil

3 shallots, finely chopped

500 g/1 lb 2 oz baby spinach leaves

4 tbsp single cream

freshly grated nutmeg

4 large eggs

4 tbsp finely grated Parmesan cheese

pepper

toasted Granary bread, to serve

Parma Ham with Figs
10 minutes to the table

SERVES 4

ingredients

175 g/6 oz thinly sliced Parma ham
4 fresh ripe figs
1 lime
2 fresh basil sprigs
pepper

method

Using a sharp knife, trim the visible fat from the slices of ham and discard. Arrange the ham on 4 large serving plates, loosely folding it so that it falls into decorative shapes. Season to taste with pepper.

Using a sharp knife, cut each fig lengthways into 4 wedges. Arrange a fig on each serving plate. Cut the lime into 6 wedges, put a wedge on each plate and reserve the remaining wedges. Remove the leaves from the basil sprigs and divide between the plates. Cover and leave to chill in the refrigerator until ready to serve.

Just before serving, remove the plates from the refrigerator and squeeze the juice from the remaining lime wedges over the ham.

variations

This dish is also delicious made with 4 slices of Charentais melon or 12–16 cooked and cooled asparagus spears instead of the figs.

Nachos
20 minutes to the table

method

Preheat the oven to 200°C/400°F/Gas Mark 6.

Spread the tortilla chips out over the base of a large, shallow ovenproof dish or roasting tin. Cover with the refried beans. Sprinkle over the chillies and pimientos and season to taste with salt and pepper. Mix the grated cheeses together in a bowl and sprinkle on top.

Bake in the preheated oven for 5-8 minutes until the cheese is bubbling and melted.

Serve immediately with guacamole and soured cream.

SERVES 6

ingredients

175 g/6 oz tortilla chips

400 g/14 oz canned refried beans, warmed

2 tbsp finely chopped bottled jalapeño chillies

200 g/7 oz canned or bottled pimientos or roasted peppers, drained and finely sliced

115 g/4 oz Gruyère cheese, grated

115 g/4 oz Cheddar cheese, grated

salt and pepper

TO SERVE

guacamole

soured cream

Scrambled Eggs with Asparagus

15 minutes to the table

method

Melt half the butter in a frying pan over a medium heat. Add the asparagus and mushrooms and cook, stirring frequently, for 5 minutes, or until softened. Remove from the frying pan, drain if necessary and keep warm.

Meanwhile, beat the eggs with the cream, adding salt and pepper to taste.

Melt the remaining butter in a non-stick saucepan over a medium heat. Pour in the egg mixture and cook, stirring gently with a wooden spoon, for 5-6 minutes, or until lightly set.

Arrange the ham on serving plates and top with the asparagus and mushrooms, then the egg mixture. Sprinkle with the chives and serve immediately.

SERVES 4

ingredients

55 g/2 oz unsalted butter

115 g/4 oz fresh baby asparagus
   spears, diagonally sliced

85 g/3 oz button mushrooms, sliced

4 eggs

3 tbsp single cream

4 thick slices lean ham

salt and pepper

1-2 tbsp snipped fresh chives, to
   garnish

Chapter Two
Main Courses

Chicken with Smoked Ham and Parmesan

30 minutes to the table

SERVES 4

ingredients

4 skinless, boneless chicken breasts
2 tbsp plain flour
55 g/2 oz unsalted butter
8 thin slices smoked ham, trimmed
55 g/2 oz freshly grated Parmesan
   cheese
salt and pepper
sprigs of fresh basil, to garnish
   (optional)

method

Cut each chicken breast through the thickness of the flesh and open out to become two separate pieces. Put the pieces between 2 sheets of clingfilm and pound with the flat end of a meat mallet or the side of a rolling pin until the chicken is as thin as possible. Spread the flour out on a shallow plate and season to taste with salt and pepper. Coat the chicken pieces in the seasoned flour, shaking off any excess.

Melt half the butter in a large, heavy-based frying pan over a medium heat. Add the chicken pieces and cook, turning frequently, for 10–15 minutes until golden brown all over and cooked through.

Meanwhile, melt the remaining butter in a small saucepan. Remove the frying pan containing the chicken from the heat. Put a slice of ham on each piece of chicken and sprinkle with the Parmesan cheese. Drizzle the melted butter over the dressed chicken, return the frying pan to the heat and cook for 3–4 minutes until the cheese has melted. Serve immediately, garnished with basil sprigs, if desired.

variation

Instead of the chicken breasts being cut and opened out, they can be slit to make a pocket and then filled with slices of smoked ham or prosciutto and fontina cheese before frying.

Pepper Steak
20 minutes to the table

SERVES 4

ingredients

2 tbsp black or mixed dried
   peppercorns, coarsely crushed
4 fillet steaks, about 2.5 cm/1 inch
   thick, at room temperature
15 g/½ oz butter
1 tsp sunflower oil
4 tbsp brandy
4 tbsp crème fraîche or double cream
   (optional)
salt and pepper
watercress leaves, to garnish
French fries, to serve

method

Spread the crushed peppercorns out on a plate and press the steaks into them to coat on both sides.

Melt the butter with the oil in a large sauté or frying pan over a medium-high heat. Add the steaks in a single layer and cook for 3 minutes on each side for rare; 3½ minutes on each side for medium-rare; 4 minutes on each side for medium; and 4½-5 minutes on each side for well done.

Transfer the steaks to a warmed plate and set aside, covering with foil to keep warm. Pour the brandy into the pan, increase the heat and use a wooden spoon to scrape any sediment from the base of the pan. Continue boiling until reduced to around 2 tablespoons.

Stir in any accumulated juices from the steaks. Spoon in the crème fraîche, if using, and continue boiling until the sauce is reduced by half again. Taste and adjust the seasoning, if necessary. Spoon the sauce over the steaks, garnish with watercress and serve immediately with French fries.

cook's tip

To crush the peppercorns coarsely, put them in a thick polythene bag and bash with the side of a rolling pin. Alternatively, use a pestle and mortar, but take care not to grind them too finely.

Steak in Orange Sauce

15 minutes to the table

method

Using a zester, pare a few strips of orange zest from 1 orange and reserve for the garnish. Cut the oranges in half, then cut off 4 thin slices and reserve for the garnish. Squeeze the juice from the remaining halves and set aside.

Melt the butter in a heavy-based frying pan over a medium heat. Add the steaks and cook for 1–2 minutes on each side, or until browned and sealed. Transfer the steaks to a warmed plate, season to taste with salt and pepper and set aside, covering with foil to keep warm.

Pour the orange juice into the frying pan and add the stock and balsamic vinegar. Simmer over a low heat for 2 minutes. Season the orange sauce to taste with salt and pepper and return the steaks to the frying pan. Heat through gently for 2 minutes, or according to taste. Transfer to warmed serving plates and garnish with the orange slices, orange zest and parsley leaves. Serve immediately.

cook's tip

Balsamic vinegar, from Modena in Italy, is considered to be the world's oldest and finest vinegar. It is best used in simple dishes and in salad dressings, and is available from most large supermarkets.

variation

Substitute 1 tablespoon Cointreau for 1 tablespoon of the juice squeezed from the oranges at the beginning of the method.

SERVES 4

ingredients

2 large oranges
25 g/1 oz butter
4 fillet steaks, about 175 g/6 oz each,
    at room temperature
6 tbsp beef stock
1 tbsp balsamic vinegar
salt and pepper

TO GARNISH
4 thin orange slices
a few strips of orange zest
fresh flat-leaf parsley leaves

Pork Fillets with Fennel
30 minutes to the table

SERVES 4

ingredients

450 g/1 lb pork fillet

2–3 tbsp virgin olive oil

2 tbsp Sambuca

1 large fennel bulb, sliced, fronds
reserved for garnish

85 g/3 oz Gorgonzola cheese,
crumbled

2 tbsp single cream

1 tbsp chopped fresh sage

1 tbsp chopped fresh thyme

salt and pepper

method

Trim any visible fat from the pork and cut into 5-mm/¼-inch thick slices. Put the slices between 2 sheets of clingfilm and pound gently with the flat end of a meat mallet or the side of a rolling pin until flattened slightly.

Heat 2 tablespoons of the oil in a heavy-based frying pan over a medium heat. Add the pork, in batches, and cook for 2–3 minutes on each side until cooked through and tender. Transfer to a warmed plate and keep warm while you cook the remaining pork, adding more oil to the frying pan, if necessary.

Pour the Sambuca into the frying pan, increase the heat and use a wooden spoon to scrape up any sediment from the base of the frying pan. Add the fennel and cook, stirring and turning frequently, for 3 minutes. Remove the fennel from the frying pan and keep warm.

Reduce the heat, add the Gorgonzola cheese and cream, and cook, stirring constantly, until smooth. Remove from the heat, stir in the sage and thyme and season to taste with salt and pepper.

Divide the pork and fennel between 4 warmed individual serving plates and pour over the sauce. Garnish with the reserved fennel fronds and serve immediately.

cook's tip

Do not overcrowd the frying pan when cooking the pork.

Mussels in White Wine
30 minutes to the table

SERVES 4

ingredients

4 shallots, finely chopped
3 garlic cloves, crushed
25 g/1 oz butter
300 ml/10 fl oz dry white wine
1 bouquet garni
2 kg/4 lb 8 oz live mussels, scrubbed
    and debearded
salt and pepper
2 tbsp chopped fresh parsley, to
    garnish

method

Using a sharp knife, finely chop the shallots, then crush the garlic. Set aside. Discard any mussels with broken shells or any that refuse to close when tapped.

Melt the butter in a large saucepan over a low heat. Add the shallots and garlic and cook, stirring frequently, for 5 minutes, or until the shallots are softened. Pour in the wine, add the bouquet garni and season to taste with salt and pepper. Bring to the boil over a medium heat and add the mussels. Cover and cook, shaking the saucepan frequently, for 3–4 minutes, or until the mussels have opened. Discard any mussels that remain closed.

Remove and discard the bouquet garni. Using a slotted spoon, divide the mussels between 4 soup bowls. Tilt the saucepan and spoon a little of the cooking liquid over each plate. Sprinkle with the parsley and serve immediately.

variation

For moules marinière Normandy-style, substitute a good-quality dry cider for the wine. Replace the bouquet garni with sprigs of thyme and a bay leaf.

Mixed Seafood Curry
30 minutes to the table

method

Using a sharp knife, finely chop the shallots, then crush the garlic. Set aside. Discard any mussels with broken shells or any that refuse to close when tapped.

Heat the oil in a preheated wok or large frying pan over a medium-high heat. Add the shallots, galangal and garlic and stir-fry for 1-2 minutes until softened. Add the coconut milk, lemon grass, fish sauce and chilli sauce. Bring to the boil, then reduce the heat and simmer for 1-2 minutes.

Add the prawns, squid, salmon and tuna and simmer for 3 minutes, or until the prawns have turned pink and the fish is just cooked.

Add the mussels, cover and simmer for 3 minutes, or until they have opened. Discard any mussels that remain closed.

Serve immediately, garnished with Chinese chives and accompanied with cooked rice.

SERVES 4

ingredients

1 tbsp vegetable or groundnut oil

3 shallots, finely chopped

2.5-cm/1-inch piece fresh galangal, thinly sliced

2 garlic cloves, finely chopped

400 ml/14 fl oz canned coconut milk

2 lemon grass stalks, snapped in half

4 tbsp Thai fish sauce

2 tbsp chilli sauce

225 g/8 oz raw tiger prawns, peeled and deveined

225 g/8 oz baby squid, cleaned and thickly sliced

225 g/8 oz salmon fillet, skinned and cut into chunks

175 g/6 oz tuna steak, cut into chunks

225 g/8 oz live mussels, scrubbed and debearded

fresh Chinese chives, to garnish

rice, to serve

Grilled Tuna and Vegetable Kebabs

25 minutes to the table

method

If using wooden skewers, presoak them in cold water for 30 minutes to prevent them burning.

Preheat the grill to high. Cut the tuna into 2.5-cm/1-inch cubes. Peel the onions, leaving the root intact, and cut each onion lengthways into 6 wedges.

Divide the tuna and vegetables evenly between 8 skewers and arrange on the grill rack.

Mix the oregano and oil together in a small bowl. Season to taste with pepper. Lightly brush the kebabs with the oil mixture and cook under the preheated grill, turning occasionally, for 10–15 minutes until evenly cooked.

Garnish with lime wedges and serve with a selection of salads and cooked couscous, new potatoes or bread.

cook's tip

These kebabs can also be cooked on a barbecue.

SERVES 4

ingredients

4 tuna steaks, about 140 g/5 oz each

2 red onions

12 cherry tomatoes

1 red pepper, deseeded and cut into 2.5-cm/1-inch pieces

1 yellow pepper, deseeded and cut into 2.5-cm/1-inch pieces

1 courgette, sliced

1 tbsp chopped fresh oregano

4 tbsp olive oil

pepper

lime wedges, to garnish

TO SERVE

selection of salads

cooked couscous, new potatoes or bread

Fettuccine with Ricotta

15 minutes to the table

method

Bring a large, heavy-based saucepan of lightly salted water to the boil.
Add the pasta, return to the boil and cook for 8-10 minutes, or until
tender but still firm to the bite. Drain well and return to the saucepan.
Add the butter and chopped parsley, reserving a few leaves for a
garnish, and toss thoroughly to coat.

Mix the ricotta cheese, ground almonds and crème fraîche together
in a bowl. Gradually stir in the oil, followed by the hot chicken stock.
Add the nutmeg and season to taste with pepper.

Transfer the pasta to a warmed serving dish, pour over the sauce and
toss to mix. Sprinkle with the pine kernels, garnish with parsley leaves
and serve immediately.

cook's tip

It is important that you mix the ricotta, ground almonds and crème
fraîche into a smooth paste before adding the oil to the sauce. Equally,
don't add the stock until the oil has been completely absorbed.

variation

To give a sharp, piquant flavour to the sauce, mix the finely grated rind
and juice of ½ lemon with the ricotta cheese, ground almonds and
crème fraîche.

SERVES 4

ingredients

350 g/12 oz dried fettuccine
40 g/1 ½ oz unsalted butter
2 tbsp chopped fresh
   flat-leaf parsley
115 g/4 oz ricotta cheese
115 g/4 oz ground almonds
150 ml/5 fl oz crème fraîche
2 tbsp extra-virgin olive oil
125 ml/4 fl oz hot chicken stock
pinch of freshly grated nutmeg
salt and pepper

TO GARNISH
1 tbsp pine kernels
a few leaves of chopped fresh
   flat-leaf parsley

Special Cauliflower Cheese

30 minutes to the table

SERVES 4

ingredients

1 cauliflower, about 675 g/1 lb 8 oz
 prepared weight, trimmed and
 broken into florets
1 tbsp olive oil
1 onion, thinly sliced
1 garlic clove, finely chopped
115 g/4 oz streaky bacon,
 cut into 1-cm/½-inch strips
3 tbsp butter
3 tbsp plain flour
425 ml/15 fl oz milk
115 g/4 oz Cheddar cheese, finely
 grated
a good grating of nutmeg
1 tbsp freshly grated Parmesan
 cheese
salt and pepper

TO SERVE
tomato or green salad
fresh crusty bread

method

Preheat the oven to 160°C/325°F/Gas Mark 3. Put an ovenproof serving dish in the oven to warm. Cook the cauliflower in a saucepan of boiling salted water for 4–5 minutes – it should still be firm. Drain and transfer to the warmed serving dish, then keep warm in the oven.

 Heat the oil in a frying pan over a medium heat. Add the onion, garlic and bacon and cook, stirring occasionally, for 10 minutes, or until the onion is caramelized and golden and the bacon is crisp.

 Meanwhile, melt the butter in a small, heavy-based saucepan over a medium heat. Stir in the flour until well combined and smooth. Cook, stirring constantly, for 1 minute. Remove from the heat and stir in a little of the milk until well incorporated. Return to the heat and gradually add the remaining milk, stirring constantly. Cook, stirring, for a further 3 minutes, or until the sauce is smooth and thickened. Remove from the heat and stir in the Cheddar cheese, nutmeg and salt and pepper to taste.

 Preheat the grill to high. Spoon the onion and bacon mixture over the cauliflower and pour over the hot sauce. Sprinkle with the Parmesan cheese and cook under the preheated grill until browned. Serve immediately with a tomato or green salad and crusty bread.

Vegetable Chop Suey
15 minutes to the table

method

Heat the oil in a preheated wok or large frying pan over a high heat until it is almost smoking. Add the onion and garlic and stir-fry for 30 seconds.

Add the peppers, broccoli, courgette, beans and carrot to the wok and stir-fry for 2–3 minutes.

Stir in the beansprouts, sugar, soy sauce and vegetable stock and toss to combine thoroughly. Season to taste with salt and pepper and cook, stirring, for a further 2 minutes.

Transfer the vegetables to warmed serving plates and serve immediately with noodles.

cook's tip

The clever design of a wok, with its spherical base and high sloping sides, enables the food to be tossed so that it is cooked quickly and evenly. It is essential to heat the wok sufficiently before you add the ingredients to ensure quick and even cooking.

SERVES 4

ingredients

2 tbsp groundnut oil
1 onion, chopped
3 garlic cloves, chopped
1 green pepper, deseeded and diced
1 red pepper, deseeded and diced
75 g/2¾ oz broccoli florets
1 courgette, sliced
25 g/1 oz French beans
1 carrot, cut into matchsticks
100 g/3½ oz fresh beansprouts
2 tsp soft light brown sugar
2 tbsp light soy sauce
125 ml/4 fl oz vegetable stock
salt and pepper
noodles, to serve

Spaghetti with Garlic and Olive Oil

15 minutes to the table

SERVES 4

ingredients

450 g/1 lb dried spaghetti
125 ml/4 fl oz extra-virgin olive oil
3 garlic cloves, finely chopped
3 tbsp chopped fresh
   flat-leaf parsley
salt and pepper

method

Bring a large, heavy-based saucepan of lightly salted water to the boil.
Add the pasta, return to the boil and cook for 8–10 minutes, or until
tender but still firm to the bite.

   Meanwhile, heat the oil in a heavy-based frying pan over a low heat.
Add the garlic and a pinch of salt and cook, stirring constantly, for 3–4
minutes, or until golden. Do not allow the garlic to brown or it will taste
bitter. Remove from the heat.

   Drain the pasta and transfer to a warmed serving dish. Pour in the
garlic-flavoured oil, then add the parsley and season to taste with salt
and pepper. Toss well and serve immediately.

cook's tip

Cooked pasta gets cold quickly, so make sure that the serving dish is
warmed thoroughly. As soon as the pasta is drained, transfer to the
dish, pour over the garlic-flavoured oil, toss and serve.

Chapter Three
Accompaniments and Light Meals

Garlic Bread
25 minutes to the table

SERVES 4-6

ingredients

1 baguette

115 g/4 oz butter, softened

6-8 garlic cloves, finely chopped

2 tsp finely grated lemon rind
(optional)

2 tbsp chopped fresh herbs, such as
parsley, thyme or chives, or
a mixture

method

Preheat the oven to 200°C/400°F/Gas Mark 6. Slice the baguette diagonally without cutting all the way through.

Beat the butter in a bowl until creamy, then beat in the garlic, lemon rind, if using, and herbs. Alternatively, melt the butter in a small saucepan, then stir in the remaining ingredients.

Spread or brush the butter onto both sides of the bread slices. Put the baguette on a large sheet of foil. If there is any butter mixture remaining, dot or pour it over the top of the loaf. Bring up the long sides of the foil and fold together to enclose the loaf. Transfer to a baking sheet and bake in the preheated oven for 15 minutes. Unwrap, cut into separate slices and serve immediately.

Sautéed Potatoes
30 minutes to the table

method

Bring a large saucepan of salted water to the boil over a high heat. Add the potatoes and, as soon as the water returns to the boil, drain well, then pat the potatoes completely dry with kitchen paper.

Melt the clarified butter (ghee) in a large sauté or frying pan with a tight-fitting lid over a medium-high heat. You only want a thin layer of butter, about 3 mm/⅛ inch deep, so, depending on the size of the pan, pour off and reserve any excess.

Add the potatoes and cook, turning frequently, for 4 minutes, or until golden all over. Add a little of the reserved clarified butter, if necessary.

Reduce the heat to very low, cover and cook, shaking the pan occasionally, for 15-20 minutes until the potatoes are golden brown and offering no resistance when pierced with a knife. Add salt and pepper to taste, then stir in the parsley.

cook's tip

Cooking potatoes in butter gives them a rich flavour, but ordinary butter would probably burn before it becomes hot enough to crisp them up, which is why clarified butter is specified, as it can be heated to a higher temperature without burning. To make clarified butter, melt unsalted butter in a small, heavy-based saucepan over a low heat until foaming. Skim off the foam from the surface, then drain off the clear (clarified) butter, leaving the milky residue behind. Alternatively, use 40 g/1½ oz unsalted butter with 1 tablespoon sunflower oil.

SERVES 4-6

ingredients

900 g/2 lb waxy potatoes, such as
    Charlotte, peeled and cut
    into chunks
55 g/2 oz clarified butter
    (see cook's tip)
salt and pepper
chopped fresh flat-leaf parsley or
    spring onions, to garnish

Warm Potatoes with Pesto

25 minutes to the table

method

Cook the potatoes in a saucepan of salted boiling water for
15 minutes, or until tender. Drain, transfer to a salad bowl and leave to
cool slightly.

Add the pesto sauce and salt and pepper to taste to the potatoes and
toss thoroughly to coat. Sprinkle with the Parmesan cheese and
serve immediately.

cook's tip

Pesto sauce, originally from Genoa in Italy, is made with fresh basil,
pine kernels, garlic, Parmesan cheese and olive oil. You can buy good
quality, fresh pesto in supermarkets.

SERVES 4

ingredients

450 g/1 lb small new potatoes

3 tsp pesto sauce

25 g/1 oz freshly grated Parmesan
  cheese

salt and pepper

Asparagus with Melted Butter

10 minutes to the table

method

Bring a large saucepan of salted water to the boil. Meanwhile, remove some of the base of the thicker asparagus stalks with a potato peeler. Tie the stalks together with clean string or use a wire basket so that they can easily be removed from the saucepan without damage.

Plunge the stalks into the boiling water, cover and cook for 4–5 minutes. Pierce a stalk near the base with a sharp knife. If fairly soft, remove the saucepan from the heat immediately. Do not overcook asparagus or the tender tips will fall off.

Drain the asparagus thoroughly and serve on large, warmed plates with the melted butter poured over. Both the butter and the asparagus should be warm rather than hot. Serve with the salt and pepper, and hand out large napkins!

variations

To griddle asparagus, brush a griddle pan with oil and then heat until it is very hot. Add the asparagus and cook for 2 minutes on one side, then turn over and cook for a further 2 minutes. Serve immediately. Asparagus is also delicious served with slices of Parma ham, fresh shavings of Parmesan cheese or soft-boiled quail's eggs. Alternatively, fry 55 g/2 oz fresh white breadcrumbs in 40 g/1½ oz butter until golden and crisp and serve scattered over lightly cooked asparagus.

SERVES 2

ingredients

16–20 fresh asparagus spears, trimmed to about 20 cm/8 inches in length
85 g/3 oz unsalted butter, melted
sea salt and pepper

Warm Pasta Salad
20 minutes to the table

SERVES 4

ingredients

225 g/8 oz dried farfalle or other
    pasta shapes
6 pieces sun-dried tomato in oil,
    drained and chopped
4 spring onions, chopped
55 g/2 oz rocket, shredded
½ cucumber, deseeded and diced
2 tbsp freshly grated Parmesan
    cheese
salt and pepper

DRESSING
4 tbsp olive oil
½ tsp caster sugar
1 tbsp white wine vinegar
1 tsp Dijon mustard
4 fresh basil leaves,
    finely shredded
salt and pepper

method

Bring a large, heavy-based saucepan of lightly salted water to the boil.
Add the pasta, return to the boil and cook for 8–10 minutes, or until
tender but still firm to the bite.

Meanwhile, to make the dressing, whisk the oil, sugar, vinegar and
mustard together in a bowl. Season to taste with salt and pepper. Stir
in the basil.

Drain the pasta and transfer to a salad bowl. Add the dressing and
toss thoroughly to coat.

Add the sun-dried tomatoes, spring onions, rocket and cucumber,
season to taste with salt and pepper and toss well. Sprinkle with the
Parmesan cheese and serve warm.

cook's tip

It is easier to toss the pasta if you use 2 forks or 2 tablespoons, and
before adding the dressing to the salad, whisk it again until emulsified.
Add the dressing just before serving.

Salade Niçoise
30 minutes to the table

SERVES 4-8

ingredients

2 tuna steaks, about 2 cm/¾ inch
    thick
olive oil, for brushing
250 g/9 oz French beans
2 lettuce hearts, leaves separated
3 large hard-boiled eggs, quartered
2 juicy vine-ripened tomatoes, cut
    into wedges
50 g/1¾ oz anchovy fillets in oil,
    drained
55 g/2 oz Niçoise olives
salt and pepper
torn fresh basil leaves, to garnish
French bread, to serve

DRESSING

125 ml/4 fl oz extra-virgin olive oil
3 tbsp white wine vinegar or lemon
    juice
1-2 garlic cloves, crushed, to taste
1 tsp Dijon mustard
½ tsp caster sugar

method

Heat a ridged, cast-iron griddle pan over a high heat until you can feel the heat rising from the surface. Brush the tuna steaks with oil, add, oiled-side down, to the griddle pan and cook for 2 minutes.

Lightly brush the top side of the tuna steaks with a little more oil. Use a pair of tongs to turn the tuna steaks over, then season to taste with salt and pepper. Cook for a further 2 minutes for rare or up to 4 minutes for well done. Leave to cool.

Meanwhile, bring a saucepan of salted water to the boil. Add the beans, return to the boil and cook for 3 minutes, or until tender-crisp. Drain and immediately transfer to a large bowl. Put all the ingredients for the dressing in a screw-top jar, screw on the lid and shake vigorously until an emulsion forms. Pour the dressing over the beans and stir together. Leave the beans to cool in the dressing.

To serve, line a platter with lettuce leaves. Lift the beans out of the bowl, leaving the excess dressing behind, and pile in the centre of the platter. Break the tuna into large flakes and arrange over the beans.

Arrange the hard-boiled eggs and tomatoes around the side and the anchovy fillets over the salad, then add the olives and basil. Drizzle the remaining dressing in the bowl over everything and serve with plenty of French bread for mopping up the dressing.

Caesar Salad
15 minutes to the table

SERVES 4

ingredients

1 large egg

2 Cos lettuces or 3 Little Gem
   lettuces, leaves separated

6 tbsp olive oil

2 tbsp lemon juice

8 canned anchovy fillets, drained
   and roughly chopped

85 g/3 oz fresh Parmesan
   cheese shavings

salt and pepper

GARLIC CROUTONS

4 tbsp olive oil

2 garlic cloves, finely chopped

5 slices white bread, crusts removed,
   cut into 1-cm/½-inch cubes

method

Bring a small, heavy-based saucepan of water to the boil.

Meanwhile, to make the croûtons, heat the oil in a heavy-based frying pan over a medium-high heat. Add the garlic and bread cubes and cook, stirring and tossing frequently, for 4–5 minutes, or until the bread is crisp and golden all over. Remove with a slotted spoon and drain on kitchen paper.

While the bread is frying, add the egg to the boiling water and cook for 1 minute, then remove and set aside.

Arrange the lettuce leaves in a salad bowl. Mix the oil and lemon juice together in a bowl, then season to taste with salt and pepper. Crack the egg into the dressing and whisk thoroughly until blended. Pour the dressing over the lettuce leaves, toss well, then add the croûtons and anchovies and toss the salad again. Sprinkle with the Parmesan cheese shavings and serve.

caution

Recipes using very lightly cooked eggs should be avoided by infants, the elderly, pregnant women, convalescents and anyone suffering from an illness.

cook's tip

Don't leave the salad standing around too long after the dressing has been added or the lettuce will go soggy and the salad will be unusable.

Mixed Seafood Salad
20 minutes to the table

method

Discard any mussels with broken shells or any that refuse to close when tapped. Heat 1 tablespoon of oil in a preheated wok or large frying pan over a high heat. Add the onion, squid, prawns and mussels and stir-fry for 2 minutes, or until the squid is opaque and the mussels have opened. Discard any mussels that remain closed.

Meanwhile, mix the spring onions, lemon grass, red pepper and Chinese leaves together in a bowl. Add the seafood and stir gently together. Turn into a serving dish.

For the dressing, mix the garlic, 2 tablespoons of oil, fish sauce, sugar and lemon juice together in a small bowl. Stir in the cucumber and tomato, spoon the dressing over the salad and seafood and serve immediately.

SERVES 4

ingredients

500 g/1 lb 2 oz live mussels, scrubbed and debearded
1 tbsp vegetable or groundnut oil
1 small onion, thinly sliced
225 g/8 oz baby squid, cleaned and sliced
225 g/8 oz cooked prawns, peeled and deveined
bunch of spring onions, roughly chopped
1 lemon grass stalk, outer leaves removed, finely chopped
1 red pepper, deseeded and cut into strips
½ small head Chinese leaves, shredded

DRESSING

2 garlic cloves, crushed
2 tbsp vegetable or groundnut oil
1 tsp Thai fish sauce
1 tsp palm sugar or soft light brown sugar
juice of 1 lemon
5-cm/2-inch piece cucumber, chopped
1 tomato, deseeded and chopped

Walnut, Pear and Crispy Bacon Salad

25 minutes to the table

method

Preheat the grill to high. Arrange the bacon on a grill rack and cook under the preheated grill until well browned and crisp. Leave to cool, then cut into 1-cm/ ½-inch pieces.

Meanwhile, heat a dry frying pan over a medium heat. Add the walnuts and dry-fry, shaking the pan frequently, for 3 minutes, or until lightly browned. Leave to cool.

Toss the pears in the lemon juice to prevent discoloration. Transfer the watercress, walnuts, pears and bacon to a salad bowl.

To make the dressing, whisk the oil, lemon juice and honey together in a small bowl or jug. Season to taste with salt and pepper, then pour over the salad. Toss well to combine and serve immediately.

SERVES 4

ingredients

4 lean back bacon rashers
75 g/2 ¾ oz walnut halves
2 Red William pears, cored and sliced
    lengthways
1 tbsp lemon juice
175 g/6 oz watercress, tough stalks
    removed

DRESSING
3 tbsp extra-virgin olive oil
2 tbsp lemon juice
½ tsp clear honey
salt and pepper

Chapter Four
Desserts

Strawberry Baked Alaska

20 minutes to the table

SERVES 6

ingredients

23-cm/9-inch round sponge cake

2 tbsp sweet sherry or orange juice

5 egg whites

140 g/5 oz caster sugar

600 ml/1 pint strawberry ice cream

175 g/6 oz fresh strawberries, hulled
and halved, plus whole
strawberries, to serve

method

Preheat the oven to 240°C/475°F/Gas Mark 9. Put the sponge cake in a large, shallow, ovenproof dish and sprinkle with the sherry.

Whisk the egg whites in a spotlessly clean, grease-free bowl until stiff. Continue to whisk, gradually adding the sugar, until very stiff and glossy.

Working quickly, cover the top of the cake with the ice cream and then top with the strawberry halves. Spread the meringue over the cake, making sure that the ice cream is completely covered. Bake in the preheated oven for 3–5 minutes, or until the meringue is golden brown. Serve immediately, with whole strawberries.

cook's tip

For the perfect meringue, bring the egg whites to room temperature before whisking. It is worth noting that the fresher the eggs, the greater the volume of the meringue.

Chocolate Fondue
15 minutes to the table

SERVES 4

ingredients

225 g/8 oz plain chocolate
200 ml/7 fl oz double cream
2 tbsp brandy

TO SERVE
selection of prepared fresh fruit
white and pink marshmallows
sweet biscuits

method

Break the chocolate into small pieces and put in a small saucepan with the cream. Heat the mixture over a low heat, stirring constantly, until the chocolate has melted and blended with the cream.

Remove from the heat and stir in the brandy.

Pour the mixture into a fondue pot or small, flameproof dish and keep warm over a small burner.

Serve with a selection of prepared fresh fruit (see cook's tip), marshmallows and biscuits for dipping. The fruit and marshmallows can be spiked on fondue forks, wooden skewers or ordinary forks for dipping into the chocolate fondue.

cook's tip

To prepare the fruit for dipping, cut larger fruit into bite-sized pieces. Fruit that discolours, such as bananas, apples and pears, should be dipped in a little lemon juice as soon as it is cut.

variation

Choose your favourite fruit to dip in the fondue. Kiwi fruit, banana chunks, apple pieces and strawberries go particularly well.

Grilled Peaches and Soured Cream
15 minutes to the table

method

Preheat the grill to medium. Plunge the peaches in a saucepan of boiling water for 1 minute. Remove and refresh under cold running water, then peel, halve, stone and slice. Arrange the peach slices in 4 individual flameproof dishes.

Mix the brown sugar and cinnamon together and sprinkle the mixture over the peaches. Spoon the soured cream on top, then sprinkle 1 tablespoon caster sugar over each dish.

Cook under the preheated grill for 2–3 minutes, or until the caster sugar has melted and caramelized. Serve immediately or leave to cool.

cook's tip

To stone peaches, cut vertically around the fruit, then twist each half in opposite directions to reveal the stone. Using the point of a knife, prise the stone out, remove with your fingers and discard.

SERVES 4

ingredients
4 fresh large, ripe peaches
2 tbsp soft light brown sugar
½ tsp ground cinnamon
300 ml/10 fl oz soured cream
4 tbsp caster sugar

Semolina Dessert
20 minutes to the table

SERVES 4

ingredients

6 tbsp vegetable or groundnut oil

3 cloves

3 green cardamom pods

8 tbsp coarse semolina

½ tsp ground saffron

50 g/1¾ oz sultanas

125 g/4½ oz granulated sugar

300 ml/10 fl oz water

300 ml/10 fl oz milk

single cream, to serve

TO DECORATE

25 g/1 oz desiccated coconut, toasted

25 g/1 oz chopped almonds

25 g/1 oz skinned pistachio nuts,
    chopped (optional)

method

Melt the oil in a saucepan over a medium heat.

Add the cloves and cardamom pods to the melted butter, reduce the heat and stir to mix.

Add the semolina and stir-fry until it turns a little darker.

Add the saffron, sultanas and sugar to the semolina mixture, stirring to mix well.

Pour in the water and milk and bring to the boil, stirring. Reduce the heat and simmer, stirring constantly, for 10 minutes, or until the semolina is cooked. Add a little more water if necessary.

Remove from the heat and transfer the semolina to a warmed serving dish.

Decorate with the toasted coconut, almonds and pistachio nuts, if using. Serve with a little cream drizzled over the top.

Exotic Fruit Cocktail
20 minutes to the table

SERVES 4

ingredients

2 oranges

2 large passion fruit

1 pineapple

1 pomegranate

1 banana

method

Cut 1 orange in half and squeeze the juice into a bowl, discarding any pips. Using a sharp knife, cut away all the peel and pith from the second orange. Working over the bowl to catch the juice, carefully cut the orange segments between the membranes to obtain skinless segments of fruit. Discard any pips.

Cut the passion fruit in half, scoop the flesh into a nylon sieve and, using a spoon, push the pulp and juice into the bowl of orange segments. Discard the seeds.

Using a sharp knife, cut away all the skin from the pineapple and cut the flesh lengthways into quarters. Cut away the central hard core. Cut the flesh into chunks and add to the orange and passion fruit mixture. Cover and refrigerate the fruit at this stage if you are not serving the fruit cocktail immediately.

Cut the pomegranate into quarters and, using your fingers or a teaspoon, remove the red seeds from the membrane. Cover and refrigerate until ready to serve – do not add too early to the fruit cocktail as the seeds discolour the other fruit.

Just before serving, peel and slice the banana, add to the fruit cocktail with the pomegranate seeds and mix thoroughly. Serve the fruit cocktail immediately.

Banana-stuffed Crêpes

25 minutes to the table

method

Sift the flour into a bowl and stir in the sugar. Make a well in the centre. Add the eggs and milk to the well and gradually beat into the flour mixture to form a smooth batter. Stir in the lemon rind.

Melt a little butter in a 20-cm/8-inch frying pan over a medium-high heat and pour in a quarter of the batter. Tilt the frying pan to coat the base and cook for 1–2 minutes until the underside is set. Flip the crêpe over and cook the other side for 1 minute. Slide out of the frying pan and keep warm. Repeat to make 3 more crêpes.

Slice the bananas and toss in the lemon juice in a bowl. Pour over the syrup and toss together. Fold each pancake into 4 and fill the centre with the banana mixture. Serve warm.

SERVES 4

ingredients

225 g/8 oz plain flour
2 tbsp soft light brown sugar
2 eggs
450 ml/16 fl oz milk
grated rind of 1 lemon
55 g/2 oz butter

FILLING
3 bananas
4 tbsp golden syrup
juice of 1 lemon

Fruit Kebabs
20 minutes to the table

method

Select skewers that will fit comfortably in your griddle pan. If using wooden skewers, presoak them in cold water for 30 minutes to prevent them burning.

Preheat the griddle pan over a medium heat.

Stone the fruit as necessary, or remove cores, and cut into similar-sized pieces. Small fruit may be left whole. Arrange alternating pieces on the skewers. Brush the fruit with the melted butter.

Spread the sugar out on a plate large enough to take the skewers. Mix in the cinnamon, if using. Roll the fruit kebabs in the sugar, pressing gently to coat.

Add the kebabs to the griddle pan and cook, turning occasionally, for 10 minutes, or until the sugar has melted and started to bubble. The fruit should still be firm.

Serve immediately, with crème fraîche, natural yogurt or ice cream.

SERVES 4

ingredients

450 g/1 lb assorted fresh fruit, such
    as peaches, apricots, plums, apples
    and pears
4 tbsp butter, melted
2 tbsp sugar
pinch of ground cinnamon (optional)

SERVING SUGGESTIONS
crème fraîche
natural yogurt
ice cream

Foaming Froth
20 minutes to the table

SERVES 4

ingredients

4 egg yolks
60 g/2 ¼ oz caster sugar
5 tbsp Marsala wine
amaretti biscuits, to serve

method

Whisk the egg yolks with the sugar in a heatproof bowl or, if you have one, in the top of a double saucepan for about 1 minute.

Gently whisk in the Marsala wine. Set the bowl over a saucepan of barely simmering water, or put the top of the double saucepan on its base filled with barely simmering water, and whisk vigorously for 10-15 minutes until thick, creamy and foamy.

Immediately pour into serving glasses and serve with amaretti biscuits.

caution

Recipes using very lightly cooked eggs should be avoided by infants, the elderly, pregnant women, convalescents and anyone suffering from an illness.

variations

You can use other wines, such as Champagne, Sauternes or Madeira, to flavour this dessert, or a liqueur, such as Chartreuse or Cointreau. Or try mixing white wine with brandy, rum or Maraschino.

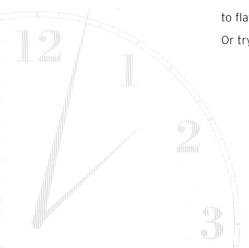

Cherry Pancakes
25 minutes to the table

method

Drain the cherries, reserving 300 ml/10 fl oz of the can juice. Put the cherries and juice in a saucepan with the almond extract and mixed spice. Stir in the cornflour until well incorporated. Bring to the boil and cook, stirring constantly, until thickened and clear. Remove from the heat and set aside.

To make the pancakes, sift the flour and salt into a bowl. Stir in the mint. Make a well in the centre. Add the egg and milk to the well and gradually beat into the flour to form a smooth batter.

Heat 1 tablespoon oil in an 18-cm/7-inch frying pan over a medium-high heat and pour off the oil when hot. Pour in a quarter of the batter. Tilt the frying pan to coat the base and cook for 1-2 minutes until the underside is set. Flip the pancake over and cook the other side for 1 minute. Slide out of the frying pan and keep warm. Repeat to make 3 more pancakes.

Spoon a quarter of the cherry mixture onto a quarter of each pancake and fold the pancake into a cone shape. Dust with icing sugar and sprinkle toasted flaked almonds over the top. Serve immediately.

SERVES 4

ingredients
400 g/14 oz canned stoned cherries
½ tsp almond extract
½ tsp ground mixed spice
2 tbsp cornflour

PANCAKES
115 g/4 oz plain flour
pinch of salt
2 tbsp chopped fresh mint
1 egg
300 ml/10 fl oz milk
vegetable oil, for frying

TO DECORATE
icing sugar
toasted flaked almonds

Index